Dedham

Constable Country

Ian St.John

In the coach yesterday coming from Suffolk,
were two gentlemen and myself,
all strangers to each other.
In passing through the valley about Dedham,
One of them remarked to me
- on my saying it was beautifull -
"Yes sir – this is Constable's country!"
I then told him who I was lest he should spoil it.
John Constable in his letter to David Lucas 14 November 1832

Suffolk Walker

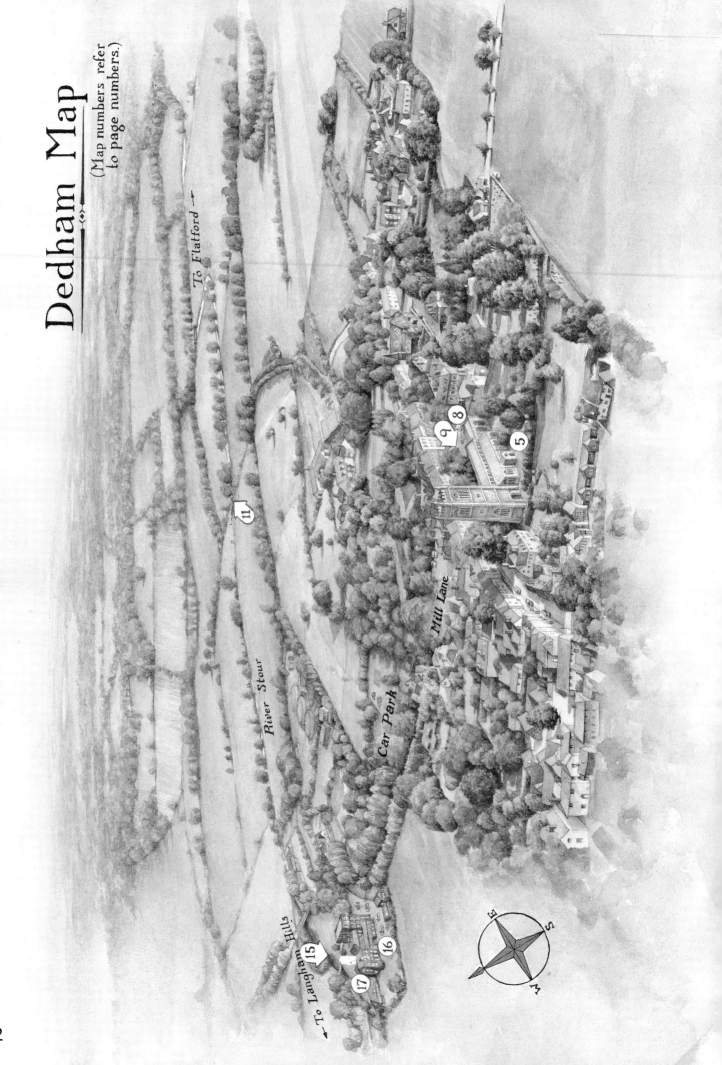

Dedham Map

(Map numbers refer to page numbers.)

To Flatford →

River Stour

Car Park

Mill Lane

To Langham Hills

Contents

Portrait of John Constable inside front cover

Dedham Map   2

 Contents   3

 Dedham Church   5

 The Altarpieces   7

 Dedham Grammar School   8

 Dedham Village   9

 The Leaping Horse   11

 River Stour Navigation   13

 Dedham Lock and Mill   15

 Dedham Mill   16

 Dedham Lock   17

Langham Hills Map   18

 Stratford St. Mary from the Coombs   19

 Stratford Mill   21

 The Glebe Farm   23

 Summer Morning   25

 Dedham Vale   27

 Dedham Vale from Gun Hill   29

 The Skylark   31

Walking in Constable Country   32

Map of Constable Country inside back cover

The map of Dedham opposite has numbers on it locating the famous views painted by John Constable. Each number on the map refers to the page in this book where you will find the corresponding painting or an interesting feature of the village. To look at the full-page landscape paintings, turn the book sideways and hold the upper page a little off vertical, as if it were on an easel, then read the text on the page below. A map of Stratford Mill and Langham hillside on page 18 is also numbered, indicating views from the Langham Hills toward Dedham.

Ambrose Waller: the landscape and Constable's art
"It was the water-meadows of the lower Stour spreading in wet, silvery acres beneath the still elms and nervous willows which caused Delacroix to sit before Constable's great landscapes and marvel. It was the beauty of this river shown in colours never before seen in landscape painting which arrested the heavy progress of early 19th century art and opened up the way to the splendours of the Impressionist movement. Now in capitals all over the world wherever the great pictures are hung, those long-past summers in the Valley are not only a landmark in the history of art, but a familiar pastoral" Ambrose J R Waller *The Suffolk Stour 1957* page 78

Dedham Church

John Constable 22 September 1815 Pencil Sketch Whereabouts unknown

Dedham Church

The large parish church of St.Mary the Virgin occupies a dominant position in the middle of the village. It was built late in the fifteenth century largely with money generated locally from the production of woollen cloth. The walls of this fine church are coated with grey cement stucco, giving prominence to the impressive flint-work of the west tower. This tower is nearly 40 metres tall, supported by strong polygonal buttresses on each corner and crowned with high, decorated pinnacles.

In the only close-up picture of the church known to have been drawn by Constable (opposite page), his focus is on the tower. A more distant Dedham Church tower features in many other Constable drawings and paintings.

A mile east of Dedham, across Dedham Vale, lays the hamlet of Flatford (see the Constable Country map inside the back cover of this book). In Constable's *A Boat Passing a Lock* (fig. 1), Dedham Church tower can be seen in the distance, framed by the stout posts of a Flatford lock gate.

The village of East Bergholt is on high ground above Dedham Vale, a mile north-east of Dedham. Flatford Lane runs from East Bergholt to Flatford. In *View of Dedham Church from Flatford Lane* (fig. 2), Dedham church tower is seen from a point just outside East Bergholt, near the junction of Flatford Lane and Fen Lane. On the lower ground in the painting is the cottage depicted in his well-known *Cottage in a Cornfield* (not shown).

Dedham from the Coombs (fig. 3) takes another stance favoured by Constable. He painted this view from the Langham Hills above Dedham Vale, about a mile west of Dedham. Views from Langham hillside are displayed in the second half of this book.

1 *A Boat passing a Lock* John Constable 1826
Oil Painting 101.6 x 127 cm (40 x 50in)
Royal Academy of Arts London

2 *View of Dedham Church from Flatford Lane*
John Constable 1802 Oil Painting
33.3 x 41.5 cm (13⅛ x 16⅜ in)
Yale Center for British Art Paul Mellon Collection

4 Dedham Church today

3 *Dedham from the Coombs* John Constable 1815
Oil Painting 48.9 x 59.7 cm (19¼ x 23½ in)
Salander-O'Reilly Galleries New York

The Risen Christ

John Constable Oil Painting 1822 160 x 127cm (63 x 50in) The Constable Trust

The Altarpieces

Constable is not widely known as a painter of religious subjects. He only painted three altarpieces which belonged to churches not far from Dedham. *The Risen Christ* (left) was painted for St.Michael's Church, Manningtree, the small Essex town three miles east of Dedham on the southern bank of the River Stour, and is currently exhibited in Dedham Church. *Christ Blessing The Elements* (fig. 5) was painted for St.James's Church, Nayland, the Suffolk village five miles west of Dedham beside the River Stour. *Christ Blessing the Children* (fig. 6) was painted for St.Michael the Archangel Church, Brantham, the Suffolk village on the northern side of the River Stour opposite Manningtree.

The Risen Christ depicts the Bible story of the Ascension of Christ where it is written that after his crucifixion and subsequent resurrection he appeared among his disciples and led them two miles out of Jerusalem to a village on the eastern slope of the mount of Olives. In the painting, Christ's open hands bear the wounds from having been nailed to the cross. He is blessing his disciples as he ascends, one of whom is seen in the bottom right-hand corner of the picture.

"And he led them out as far as to Bethany, and he lifted up his hands, and blessed them.
And it came to pass, while he blessed them, he was parted from them, and carried up into heaven".   Luke 24:50-51

Christ Blessing the Elements shows Christ during the Jewish festival of The Passover, which celebrates the angel of the Lord having passed over Jewish homes instead of killing their first-born sons. The elements Christ is blessing are the bread and wine, knowing this would be his last supper before being crucified.

"And as they were eating, Jesus took bread and blessed it, and brake it, and gave it to the disciples, and said, Take, eat; this is my body.
And he took the cup, and gave thanks. And gave it to them, saying, Drink ye all of it;
For this is my blood of the new testament, which is shed for many for the remission of sins".   Matthew 26:26-28

Christ Blessing the Children
"And they brought young children to him, that he should touch them: and his disciples rebuked those that brought them.
But when Jesus saw it, he was much displeased, and said unto them, Suffer the little children to come unto me, and forbid them not : for of such is the kingdom of God.
Verily I say unto you, Whosoever shall not receive the kingdom of God as a little child, he shall not enter therein.
And he took them up in his arms, put his hands upon them, and blessed them".   Mark 10:13-16

5 *Christ Blessing the Elements* John Constable 1810
Oil Painting 117.5 x 94cm (46¼ x 37in)
St. James's Church Nayland

6 *Christ Blessing the Children* John Constable 1805
Oil Painting 213.4 x 127cm (84 x 50in)
St Michael the Archangel Church Brantham

7 Dedham High Street in 1832 G B Campion (engraved by J C Armytage) Essex Record Office
The school is the Georgian house to the left of the group of children playing in the High Street during a break from lessons

8 Dedham Grammar School Robert Cook
Today the school buildings are private homes

Dedham Grammar School

Constable had been sent to boarding schools by his parents from perhaps the early age of seven, until his teens. As a teenager it must have given him a tremendous feeling of freedom and pleasure to be a dayboy walking across Dedham Vale from his family home at East Bergholt to Dedham Grammar School (fig. 8), and to return home in the afternoon. The school was founded during the reign of Elizabeth I in 1575 and the Reverend Dr. Thomas Letchmere Grimwood was Constable's schoolmaster.

9 *Dr Grimwood* John Constable
1805 Oil Painting
92.1 x 73.3cm (36¼ x 28⅞in)
Colchester Museums Collection

Constable's biographer, C R Leslie, who had been friends with Constable later in his life, had this to say of the relationship of master and pupil:
"Dr. Grimwood had penetration enough to discover that he was a boy of genius, although he was not remarkable for proficiency in his studies, the only thing he excelled in being penmanship. He acquired, however, some knowledge of Latin, and subsequently took private lessons in French, in which he made less progress. He was at this time sixteen or seventeen years of age, and had become devotedly fond of painting. During his French lessons a long pause would frequently occur, which his master would be the first to break, saying, 'Go on, I am not asleep: Oh! Now I see you are in your painting-room".

10 The present day view west along Dedham High Street

Dedham Village

Dedham is undoubtedly one of the most beautiful villages in Essex. The map of Dedham (looking eastwards) on page 2 shows the main village street narrowing to the church where it forms a gentle arc, with parades of interesting small shops. The street then broadens out at the centre of the village - its junction with Mill Lane and Royal Square – and continues as a wide street, lined with elegant old houses, to a bend at Dedham Hall. The village was built on a gravel river terrace, several metres above the flat alluvial vale which is susceptible to flooding in the winter months.

A house in Dedham High Street, occupied by Dame Rachel Beaumont, was where John Constable first met her son, the artist and connoisseur Sir George Beaumont. It was in this house, in about 1795, that Constable was shown an exquisite Claude painting, *Landscape with Hager and the Angel* (fig.38 on page 27), which Sir George often took with him on his travels. Constable also had the opportunity to study thirty or so Girtin watercolours belonging to Sir George Beaumont's art collection. This contact with great art affected him profoundly, and was the beginning of a new period in his life as he prepared to take lodgings in London and study fine art at the Royal Academy School.

It is perhaps surprising that there are not many pictures by Constable of the village. The eminent Constable scholar, Graham Reynolds, mentions seeing one pencil sketch by Constable of Dedham High Street believed to have been drawn the year he met Sir George Beaumont, but, regrettably, the whereabouts of this

11 *Sir George Beaumont* Thomas Lawrence
1793 or 1808 Oil Painting
Musée du Louvre Paris

The Leaping Horse

John Constable 1825 Full-scale Oil Sketch 129.4 x 188cm (51 x 74in) Victoria and Albert Museum

Constable worked simultaneously on two large oil sketches of this subject in his London studio. One of them (the full-scale oil sketch above) was laid aside. The other was removed from the supporting frame over which it had been stretched and a 2½-inch canvas strip was sewn to its top edge. Constable balanced his composition by adding a prominent tall tree to the group of trees on the left. After further work, the completed picture (page 11) was submitted to the 1825 Royal Academy Exhibition.

In this canal scene, Constable catches the dramatic moment of a lad on a horse leaping the boundary fence on Float Bridge along the River Stour towpath. They are jumping from Dedham, Essex, into East Bergholt, Suffolk. *The Leaping Horse* was the last of six large paintings Constable set on the River Stour.

12 *A Crack Willow Pollard* John Constable 1821
Pencil Sketch 9.3 x 11.9cm (3⅝ x 4¾in) Witt Collection
Courtauld Institute Galleries London

The Leaping Horse

John Constable 1825 Oil Painting 142.2 x 187.3cm (56 x 73¾in) Royal Academy of Arts London

A letter from Constable to his good friend, John Fisher, in April 1825 conveys his deep affection for the painting: *"I have worked very hard – and my large picture went last week to the Academy – but I must say that no one picture ever departed from my easel with more anxiety on my part with it. It is a lovely subject, of the canal kind, lively - & soothing – calm and exhilarating, fresh - & blowing, but it should have been on my easel a few weeks longer"*.

The idea for *The Leaping Horse* may have originated from his own tiny pencil sketch of a leaning willow pollard with Dedham Church tower (fig. 12) in the far background. He transferred this willow to the full-scale oil sketch and, although we are now looking down river towards Flatford rather than up river to Dedham, Constable kept the church tower in the picture for its good effect. He then changed and repositioned the willow in the final picture.

13 *Study for The Leaping Horse* John Constable 1825
Pencil and Grey Wash 20.3 x 30.2cm (8 x 11⅞in) British Museum
This is one of two similar pencil and grey wash sketches which were used by Constable when composing *The Leaping Horse*

14 A gang of lighters being towed away from Swan Lock c.1900 John Marriage Photograph Collection

River Stour Navigation

The spectacular series of exhibition pictures set on the River Stour help define the territory of Constable Country. The river at Flatford is the setting for four of these large paintings: *The White Horse, The Haywain, The Lock and View on the Stour near Dedham*. Between Flatford and Dedham is the site of *The Leaping Horse* (pages 10 and 11) and lastly, still further up stream, past Dedham, Constable painted *Stratford Mill* (page 20), the river scene beside the watermill at Stratford St.Mary.

The River Stour meanders eastwards, almost fifty miles from its source just inside Cambridgeshire at Weston Green, to the North Sea at Harwich. Halfway downstream it passes through the Suffolk market town of Sudbury (fig.16). Early in the eighteenth century, construction works were needed which would enable heavy cargo to be transported on the river between Sudbury and Mistley on the Stour estuary and money was raised by the Corporation of Sudbury to pay for these. Cargo was carried in Stour lighters (barges), vessels unique to the navigation and built in several dry-docks at Flatford.

Laden with about thirteen tons of goods, a lighter sank about a yard into the water. To provide sufficient water for it to float, the river was dammed in thirteen places with pound-locks (a chamber with a pair of lock gates at either end). Another two pound-locks were added along the river many years later. Thirteen staunches, also called flash-locks (single removable gates across the flow), were installed to deepen the river but later abandoned.

Often goods were transported on a pair of lighters chained together (a gang) and pulled by a horse. The tow path beside the Stour was discontinuous and required the tow horse to cross the river thirty-three times between Brantham and Sudbury. In most cases, the horse leapt on the lighter and was "boated" (ferried) across. This event was the subject of Constable's painting *The White Horse* (not shown). Tow horses also had to jump over one hundred and thirty-two stiles (one of these stiles is seen in fig. 15) along the way. In his book 'The Suffolk Stour', Ambrose Waller writes about William Cardy, who was a tow horse leader as a boy: *"The horse leader used to ride the horse most of the way, and at one time there were many stiles to jump. Cardy tells me that many is the fall that he had when trying to take the jump on the horse's back".* At the time, local people contended that had there been a Grand National for tow horses, Stour Navigation horses would have been hot favourites.

15 A gang of lighters on the Stour
c.1900 John Marriage Photograph Collection
Having leapt the fence, the horse resumes towing the gang to Wormington Lock

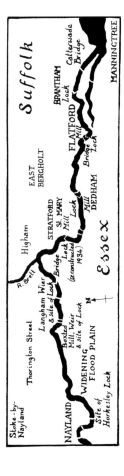

16 The River Stour Navigation from Sudbury to Catterwade Robert Cook

Dedham Lock and Mill

John Constable 1820 Oil Painting 71 x 90.2cm (28 x 35½in) Private Collection

Constable is understood to have worked in Dedham Mill for a brief spell as a young man when his father was part-owner of the mill. His inspiration for the painting *Dedham Lock and Mill* (above) came from both his affection for Dedham Mill and love for his father, Golding Constable.

Constable first drew the view of the mill and lock in 1809, the year Golding Constable is thought to have become its sole owner. In July 1816, two months after the death of his father, Constable sketched the mill again (fig. 17) and began to contemplate a finished oil painting of the scene. In preparation for this, he produced another pencil sketch (now in The Huntington, San Marino), an oil sketch (fig. 18), and an unfinished painting (in the Tate Gallery).

17 *Dedham Lock and Mill* John Constable 1816 Pencil Sketch
8.6 x 11.4cm (3⅜ x 4½in) Private Collection

Dedham Lock and Mill

John Constable 1820 Oil Painting 53.7 x 76.2cm (21⅛ x 30in) V & A Picture Library London

The mill, lock and church immediately attract our attention in *Dedham Lock and Mill* (page 14). We look, from the towpath on the Suffolk side of the River Stour, across the shimmering mill-pool towards Dedham. Sunshine has broken through burst rain clouds that are rumbling and moving off above the tall ash tree sheltering a tow-horse. Meanwhile, two rain-soaked men bring the lighter through the lock.

In a second version of *Dedham Lock and Mill* (above), a Stour lighter has been towed upstream by a chestnut tow-horse attached loosely to the towrope. Whereas the burgee at the top of the lighter mast shows the wind blowing from left to right, the full sail of the lighter in the mill headrace suggests wind coming from a different quarter and the smoke from the chimney on the mill out-building indicates the air is still!

18 *Dedham Lock and Mill* John Constable 1816
Oil Sketch 18.1 x 24.8cm (7⅛ x 9¾in)
V & A Picture Library London

Dedham Mill

19 DETAIL *Dedham Lock and Mill* John Constable 1820 Private Collection

20 Dedham Mill (Clover's Mill) Derek Tripp Photograph Collection

When mentioned in the Doomsday book the mill had one pair of millstones, which ground local corn, and a second set of stones was added to it and working by 1086.

A larger mill was built on the same site in the fifteenth century, and fulling was undertaken, a process where cloth was scoured and cleaned with fuller's earth as it was pounded by water-powered wooden hammers. Corn milling continued in the same building. Fulling and corn milling continued until 1777, when fulling ceased with the demise of local cloth production.

During the nineteenth century, the mill was replaced by the substantial brick watermill seen in the several versions of Constable's *Dedham Lock and Mill* (pages 14 and 15, and fig. 19). The wheelhouse pictured here is open-fronted, with a lean-to peg-tiled roof. The roof is shown as straight in the painting on page 14, and has an extension protecting the axle from weather in the painting on page 15. In 1764 Constable's father, Golding Constable, inherited Flatford Mill, a working watermill two miles downstream from Dedham Mill.

22 *Abram Constable* John Constable 1806
Oil Painting 76 x 63.5cm (30 x 25in)
Ipswich Museums and Galleries

21 Dedham Mill after the fire June 1908 Dedham Village Association

Twenty-four years later, Dedham Mill itself came up for sale and he bought himself a stake in it. In a 1791 trade directory, he and Mr Garrard are listed as its millers.

In 1809 Golding invested a considerable amount of money in Dedham Mill, which leads us to believe that by this time he was sole owner of the mill. His youngest son, Abram (fig. 22), was twenty-six years old and had been assisting him for a long time.
Abram Constable ran the family businesses after his father died in 1816, and managed Dedham Mill until his own retirement in 1845. By this time the mill was working five pairs of stones.

Later in the century the mill was replaced with another (fig. 20) which consisted of two brick storeys with a further four weather-boarded timber storeys above. The upper storeys were destroyed in a fire in June 1908 and the brick ruin was replaced with a new mill in 1913, which continued to work until the early 1980's. In a photograph (fig. 21), Dedham church tower is seen through the smoke, to the left of the steam mill tower.

Dedham Lock

There are several preparatory oil sketches of Dedham Lock by Constable (e.g. fig. 24), but no known finished paintings of the same. In the detail from *Dedham Lock and Mill* (fig.19) a tall post is set on each side of the entrance to the lock, topped with a galley beam. A pair of lock gates also had posts, joined by a beam to prevent them leaning in under the weight of the lock gates. Constable chose to omit these and other sets of beams from his painting, and keep the background open to view. The lock we see today (fig. 23) was built in 1838, parallel and just to the right of the lock seen in *Dedham Lock and Mill*.

23 Dedham Mill and Lock today

24 *Dedham Lock* John Constable 1820 Oil Sketch 11.5 x 16.5cm (4½ x 6½ in)
Yale Center for British Art New Haven

25 A barge party on its way through Dedham Lock *c.*1900
John Marriage Photograph Collection

Langham Hills Map

(Map numbers refer to page numbers.)

The aerial map above is of the Langham Hills. They were a favourite haunt of Constable's and extend along the south-west side of Dedham Vale. The map shows views across the vale, from above Stratford St. Mary watermill towards Langham parish church, and leftwards along the hillside to Gun Hill. The page numbers on the map locate the famous views painted by Constable.

From a letter by Constable to his wife Maria

"I have been this morning a walk up the Langham Hills, and through a number of beautiful fields & by the side of the river – and in my life I never saw Nature more lovely"

John Constable's Correspondence: The Family at East Bergholt 1801-1837 9 May 1819 page 180

Stratford St.Mary from the Coombs

John Constable 1800 Oil Painting 48 x 63.5cm (18⅞ x 25in) Private Collection

Constable was standing in a small field next to the Coombs on Dedham Vale's Langham hillside when he painted the above scene towards Stratford St.Mary, below him. Robert Cook's aerial watercolour map on page 18 looks across the same countryside but from the opposite direction: Stratford Mill to the Langham Hills.

In Constable's painting, meadows stretch out below, with people walking along the towpath next to the river. Only this time, unlike in other River Stour scenes, there are neither tow-horses on the path nor barges on the river. The tower of Stratford parish church is placed centrally, above the village and below a placid sky. To the left of the painting, beside the river, is Stratford watermill.

26 Stratford Mill from the South Stratford St. Mary Parish Council
This is an early photograph of the tall brick-built watermill which replaced the timber-framed mill seen in Constable's paintings.

Stratford Mill

John Constable 1820 Oil Painting 127 x 182.9cm (50 x 72in) National Gallery London

27 *Sketch for Stratford Mill* John Constable 1820 Oil Sketch
30.5 x 42cm (12 x 16½in) Private Collection

28 *Full-scale Oil Sketch for Stratford Mill* John Constable
1820 131 x 184cm (51½ x 72½in)
Yale Center for British Art New Haven

A corner of Stratford St.Mary watermill, with its undershot wooden wheel, is visible on the extreme left edge of the painting. The old timber-framed mill was clad with weather-boards and roofed with dark red clay peg-tiles. Our high vantage point is from an unseen footbridge (which appears in *Stratford St.Mary from the Coombs* page 19) looking down the River Stour. Three children are fishing together from a small island in front of the bridge, while another is fishing alone nearby. A clump of tall alders occupies the middle of the painting, the trees' shadows casting across the water towards the idle barge and its occupants. In 1840, three years after Constable's death, David Lucas engraved a series of paintings for Constable's book *English landscape*, which was published in parts and issued from June 1830 to July 1823. One of these engravings was of the painting *Stratford Mill* and was printed after Constable's death with the title *The Young Waltonians*, after Izaak Walton, author of the classic guide to fishing *The Compleat Angler*.

Stratford Mill was the second six-foot wide painting set on the River Stour, which Constable sent to the Royal Academy exhibition. The first was *The White Horse* (not shown), exhibited the previous year, and applauded by its critics. As usual, his method of work here was to flesh out the composition in his London studio by using preliminary pencil and oil sketches. One of these is a rapidly executed oil sketch (fig. 27) which lays out the principal features of the finished painting, and another is his six-foot wide oil sketch (fig. 28) of the scene.

The old mill seen in *Stratford Mill* was rented in 1822 by the miller William Harris from the mill owner Ebenezer Hollick. In that year a *Suffolk Chronicle* advertisement about Stratford Mill gives us a great insight into the sort of work going on at the mill at the time: *"To be let. An excellent OIL and FLOUR MILL…in Stratford St.Mary…, now belonging to, and in the. occupation of, Mr. Ebenezer Hollick, who is retiring from business The Oil Mill has one pair of stones, and one pair of rollers for crushing seed Three oil presses with going gears etc capable of pressing three thousand quarters of seed in the year. The granaries will hold two thousand quarters of seed and corn, and the leaden cisterns will hold sixty tons of oil. The Flour Mill contains two pairs of stones for grinding, and proper machinery for dressing flour, and is capable of grinding and dressing about eight hundred quarters of wheat in the year… The buildings are all in good repair"*. The measure for vegetable seed or corn is a quarter of a ton

Only five years after Constable exhibited his painting of Stratford Mill, the mill was replaced with a five-storey white-brick corn-mill (fig. 26 on page 19), and then in 1844 the mill was bought and occupied by William Back. The *Suffolk Chronicle* records, on 26 January 1861, a tragic incident in which six men were standing on the water wheel, "treading" it to free it of ice, when it suddenly moved. A man named Harris fell between the wheel and culvert and was killed instantly. The newspaper records that one of the floats on the iron breast-shot waterwheel had been bent in the accident. The mill stopped operating in 1890. Its upper storeys were demolished in 1948 leaving only the ground floor walls, which remain there to this day.

The Glebe Farm

John Constable 1827 Oil Painting 46.5 x 59.6cm (18¼ x 23½ in) Detroit Institute of Arts

The parish church of St.Mary the Virgin at Langham appears in the distance in many of Constable's Dedham Vale paintings. Only in the above picture, and versions of it, are we given a close-up of the church tower beside a farmhouse. Constable may have felt compelled to produce this work as a tribute to his friend Bishop John Fisher, who had died in 1825. The two men were first introduced to one another in 1798 by Fisher's curate and a Constable family friend, the Reverend Brooke Hurlock, when Fisher was rector *in commendam* (a living without duties) of Langham church.

Constable also became a close friend of the Bishop's nephew, Archdeacon John Fisher, to whom he described, on 9 September 1829, *The Glebe Farm: "My last landscape [is] a cottage scene – with the Church of Langham – the poor bishops first living - & which he held at Exeter in commendamus. It is one of my best – very rich in colour - & fresh and bright – and I have "pacified it" – so that is gains much by that tone & solemnity".* His painting derives from an oil sketch (fig. 29) of the farmhouse at Church Farm. In the foreground of this sketch, a peasant girl in a black cloak walks a field-edge path. In the larger oil painting, Constable widens the path into a green lane and the peasant girl now wears a red cloak. A little black and white dog has been added to the picture and is trailing behind the girl beside a pool, while to the left of the lane, two donkeys are grazing.

If this painting was intended to be a memorial to his friend Bishop Fisher, Constable did not mean to keep it for private viewing. He exhibited the finished painting at the 1827 British Institution exhibition, where it was bought by George Morant. Following this success, Constable painted several versions (not shown) of the same picture. One of these, now in the Tate Gallery, was copied by Lucas as a mezzotint entitled *The Glebe Farm* and published as such in Constable's book *English Landscape*. An unfinished version of the painting was given by Constable to his friend C R Leslie. In yet another, Constable was undecided about the composition. The church tower was changed into a windmill which was then painted out to become a church spire.

29 *Church Farm (Glebe Farm)* John Constable 1811 Oil Sketch 19.7 x 28cm (7¾ x 11in) V & A Picture Library London

30 Church Farm farmhouse and Langham Church today. The farmhouse is a splendid example of a late-medieval hall-house. Although it stands close to the church it has never been part of the church estate. Constable gave it the erroneous name Glebe Farm. He improved the composition of his painting by placing the church to the right of the farmhouse

31 *Dedham from Langham* John Constable *c.*1827 Oil Sketch 61 x 99cm (24 x 39in)
Collection René et Madeleine Junod Musée des Beaux-Arts La Chaux-de-Fonds

32 *Summer Morning* David Lucas 1831 Mezzotint Engraving 14 x 21.9cm (5½ x 8⅝in) British Museum London

Summer Morning

The panoramic view east across Dedham Vale from Hill Field (field number 572 on fig. 35) beside Langham church was a favourite of Constable's.

He made several drawings of the vista in his 1813 sketchbook and various oil sketches (e.g. figs. 33 and 34). These studies were referred to when, some years later, he painted an oil sketch of the scene on a medium-sized canvas (fig. 31), possibly as the forerunner of a projected larger picture intended to be the mirror image of *Dedham Vale: Morning* (not shown) displaying the vale from the top of Fen Lane, East Bergholt. All human activity and livestock seen on Hill Field in *Summer Morning* depict the livelihood of the tenant of Church Farm (page 23) who worked Hill Field.

The scene held such fascination for Constable that he included it in his book *English Landscape*, published in 1831, as a mezzotint by Lucas (fig. 32), with the title *Summer Morning*. Constable wrote a draft text which did not accompany the engraving, in which he says: *"Nature is never seen, in this climate at least, to greater perfection than at about 9 O'clock in the mornings of July and August when the sun has gained sufficient strength to give splendour to the Landscape 'still gemmed with the morning dew', without its oppressive heat, And it is still more delightful if vegetation has been refreshed with a shower during the night"*.

Lucas initially based his engraving of *Summer Morning* on Constable's oil sketch *Dedham from Langham* (fig. 33). In this oil sketch, the boy has cast a short shadow from the east indicating it is early morning. Various suggestions have been put forward as to what the boy is holding: a gun, flute, scythe, violin or a stick with a bottle slung from it over his shoulder. He was eventually replaced by a milkmaid and another cow was added to the scene. A later mezzotint proof incorporated a man in a white shirt leading two horses down the field, taken from another oil sketch *Dedham from Langham* (fig. 34).

There are so many similarities between the oil sketch *Dedham from Langham* in the Musée des Beaux-Arts de la Chaux-de-Fonds (fig. 31) and the published print that we can safely assume the sketch was on hand to assist Lucas.

33 *Dedham from Langham* John Constable 1812
Oil Sketch 21.6 x 30.5cm (8½ x 12in)
V & A Picture Library London

34 *Dedham from Langham* John Constable 1812
Oil Sketch 19 x 32cm (7½ x 12⅝in)
Ashmolean Museum Oxford

35 DETAIL Langham Title Map 1838 Essex Record Office

Dedham Vale

John Constable 1828 Oil Painting 145 x 122cm (57⅛ x 48in) National Gallery of Scotland Edinburgh

Dedham Vale

This view shows Dedham Vale from above the wooded hillside, later named "The Coombs", between Langham Church and Gun Hill.

During May 1802 Constable once again studied Sir George Beaumont's pictures (page 9), including Claude's *Landscape with Hager and the Angel* (fig. 38), and then wrote to his good friend John Dunthorne: *"Nature is the fountain's head, the source from whence all originally must spring ... I shall shortly return to Bergholt where I shall make some laborious studies from nature – and I shall endeavour to get a pure and unaffected representation of the scenes that may employ me with respect to colour particularly..."*.

He did visit his family home and *in situ* painted *Dedham Vale from the Coombs* (fig. 36). The influence of his study of the Claude painting (fig. 38) on the composition of this painting has long been recognised. Typically Claudian are the dark greenish-brown foreground, large trees to one side, with smaller trees on the other, and a lighter green middle distance with an expanse of water (the River Stour) and a feature, Dedham church. It was one of several studies, including *The Stour Valley with Dedham in the Distance* (fig. 37), Constable used to inform his scintillating Royal Academy exhibit *Dedham Vale*.

36 *Dedham Vale from the Coombs* John Constable 1802 Oil Painting 43.5 x 34.4cm (17⅛ x 13½in) V&A Picture Library London

38 *Landscape with Hagar and the Angel* Claude 1647 Oil Painting 52.7 x 43.8cm (23⅝ x 20¾in) National Gallery London

37 *The Stour Valley with Dedham in the Distance* John Constable 1808 Oil Painting 49.8 x 60cm (19⅝ x 23¾in) V&A Picture Library London

Constable painted this unfinished landscape part way down the hillside with the tall trees behind him. The houses in the picture still exist. On the left of Stratford Bridge, the two semi-detached cottages are now one residence. The house to the right of the bridge is today *le Talbooth* restaurant

Dedham Vale from Gun Hill

39 *Dedham Vale with Stratford St. Mary in the Distance*
John Constable 1800 Watercolour and Ink
34 x 51.7cm (13⅜ x 20⅜in) Ashmolean Museum Oxford

40 The Gun public house Colchester Museums Collection
The photograph shows the landlord Mr Parnel pushing a cart,
with his wife standing in the doorway.
On 17 March 1967 the pub closed to the public

John Constable 1813 Oil Painting 23 x 35.5cm (9⅛ x 14in) Staatsgalerie Stuttgart

In this painting we see the London to Ipswich turnpike road from a place high on Gun Hill where Constable first glimpsed his native countryside whenever he travelled from London to his family home in Suffolk. Constable was in a coach travelling on this road during 1832 when, *"passing through the valley about Dedham"* (title page), a fellow passenger remarked they were in *"Constable's country!"*.

The reclining figure by the wayside tipping his hat may perhaps represent Constable, this time travelling on foot, pausing to pay his respects to Dedham Vale, his home country. A few buttercups are in flower near the man's feet, where a worn footpath leads down into the vale. The River Stour is behind Gun Hill Cottage, with the river estuary beyond Dedham church tower. Constable had made a pencil sketch of the same scene (not illustrated) in 1805, which is now in the Royal Albert Memorial Museum, Exeter.

The Hurlock family of Dedham were old friends of the Constable family. During April 1800, Lucy Hurlock wrote a letter to John Constable supporting his determination to become a successful artist, at a time when he was receiving stinging criticism from his father who wanted him to join the family business. She wrote that she hoped to *"obtain a sight of the production of gradual progress of an early genius"*. When Lucy married a Norfolk man, Thomas Blackburn, in November of the same year at Dedham church, Constable gave her a wedding present of four watercolours, which together gave a panorama of Dedham Vale from the Essex side.

He copied one of these watercolours (fig. 39), a further view from Gun Hill, to keep for himself. This picture looked north across the vale from beside the road. A wagon with a white hood is descending the hill on its way to the toll-gate. Gun Hill was so steep that some drivers lost control of their carts going down the hill, and others were known to whip their horses mercilessly to gain the top of the hill. A poem by T. T. H. Posuit, cast in iron and on display by the tollhouse at the bottom of the hill, pleaded with drivers to rest their draught-animals part way up the hill.

THE DUMB ANIMALS HUMBLE PETITION.
REST, DRIVERS REST, ON THIS STEEP HILL,
DUMB BEASTS, PREY USE, WITH ALL GOOD WILL
GOAD NOT, SCOURGE NOT, WITH THRONGED WHIPS,
LET NOT, ONE CURSE, ESCAPE YOUR LIPS.
"GOD SEES AND HEARS"

It is perhaps a coincidence that *The Gun* inn (fig. 40) was established halfway up the hill.

The Skylark

John Constable 1830 Oil Sketch 23.7 x 20.2cm (9⅜ x 8in) Private Collection

The Skylark

Hail to thee, blithe spirit!
Bird thou never wert,
That from heaven, or near it
Pourest thy full heart
In profuse strain of unpremeditated art.

Higher still and higher
From the earth thou springest
Like a cloud of fire;
The blue deep thou wingest,
And singing still dost soar, and soaring ever singest.

From *To a Skylark* by Percy Bysshe Shelley

Constable first captured a moment in the flight of a
skylark as a pencil drawing on a page of his pocket
sketchbook, used in Essex and Suffolk between 10
July and 22 October 1813 (fig. 41). The sketchbook
was given by Constable's second daughter, Isobel, to
the V & A in 1888. Below the sketch an inscription
by the artist reads *Dedham / The Sky Lark.* Constable
was standing near a cornfield not far from Gun Hill
when he drew.

The superb oil painting *The Skylark* (opposite page)
imitates the pencil picture. Constable probably
sketched the painting in his studio, using only a
palette knife. Once again, Dedham church tower
caught his fancy. Beyond it is the River Stour
estuary while, to the left of it, Dedham Vale fields
and the River Stour can be made out.

In the pencil sketch, the lark is low in the sky,
whereas in the oil painting, it has flown *"Higher still
and higher"*. Skylarks are exuberant little birds the size
of a common sparrow, greyish, streaked with brown,
and with a white belly. They remain common in the
Dedham Vale and are seen flying as high as 150
metres, singing as they climb until just specks in the
sky; they hover for up to five minutes, singing a
clear, continuous and loud warbling song, and still
sing as they descend to the ground. The air may be
full of the sound of many larks singing from dawn
to dusk.

In *A Summerland* (fig.42) Constable paints another
bird hovering in the sky. This time it is on the
opposite side of Dedham Vale on the East Bergholt
hillside. It appears to be a bird of prey such as a
kestrel or sparrowhawk, birds still common in the
vale.

41 *Dedham / The Sky Lark* John Constable 1813 Pencil Sketch
8.9 x 12cm (3½ x 4¾in) V & A Picture Library London

42 *A Summerland* John Constable 1824 Oil Painting
42.5 x 76cm (16¾ x 30in) Yale Center for British Art

Walking in Constable Country

Walking through 'Constable Country' could not be easier. As you arrive at Manningtree railway station, the view from the platform is across Cattawade Marshes nature reserve. Dedham is only three miles (5km) away. Follow the path marked on the Constable Country map (opposite page). The walk takes you along tracks to the River Stour and along the top of the river embankment to a flood barrier. Turn left by the barrier and, for guidance, follow the footpath signs, the map and the tower of Dedham Church in the distance.

Manningtree railway station is the 'Gateway to Constable Country'. It is the main-line station, less than an hour from London (Liverpool Street) and from Norwich. It is accessible from Cambridge via Ipswich, and from the continent via Harwich. As well as providing easy access to Dedham, Flatford and East Bergholt, the station is the starting place for adventurous long walks through Essex and Suffolk. These paths are the Essex Way, Painter's Way, St.Edmund Way, Stour Valley Path, Suffolk Coast and Heaths Path, and Suffolk Way. Dedham is a most attractive village with shops and places to eat which you are sure to enjoy.

Further Reading

Lucy Archer *Dedham Visitor's Guide* Loom House 2004
R B Beckett (ed) *John Constable's Correspondence* Suffolk Records Society 1962-1968
Volume 1 *The Family at East Bergholt 1801-1837*
Volume 2 *Early Friends and Maria Bicknell (Mrs Constable)*
Volume 3 *The Correspondence with C R Leslie RA*
Volume 4 *Patrons, Dealers and Fellow Artists*
Volume 5 *Various Friends, with Charles Boner and the Artist's children*
Volume 6 *The Fishers*
R B Beckett *John Constable Discourses* Suffolk Records Society 1970
The Bible King James Version 1873
John H H Griffin *The Village of Stratford St.Mary and its Church* 1964
Charles R Leslie *Memoirs of the life of John Constable RA* 1843 Jonathan Mayne (Ed) Phaidon 1951
Gerard G Moate *Dedham Parish Church*
Francis Morgan Nichols (and Charles Alfred Jones) *A History of Dedham* Wiles & Son 1907
Felicity Owen and David Blayney Brown *Collector of Genius: A life of Sir George Beaumont* Yale UP 1988
Leslie Parris and Ian Fleming-Williams *Constable* Tate Gallery 1991
Leslie Parris, Conal Shields and Ian Fleming-Williams *John Constable Further Documents and Correspondence* Suffolk Records Society 1975
Leslie Parris, Ian Fleming-Williams and Conal Shields *Constable: Paintings, Watercolours & Drawings* Tate 1976
Nicolas Peglitsis *Sketches of Dedham Vale as John Constable saw it* CPRE 1982
George Pluckwell *John Constable's Essex* Ian Henry Publications 1987
Gerald H Rendall *Dedham Described and Deciphered*
Graham Reynolds *The Early Paintings and Drawings of John Constable* Yale University Press 1996
Graham Reynolds *The Later Paintings and Drawings of John Constable* Yale University Press 1984
Michael Rosenthal *Constable: The Painter and his Landscape* Yale University Press 1983
Ian St.John *East Bergholt Constable Country* Suffolk Walker 2002
Ian St.John *Flatford Constable Country* Suffolk Walker 2000
Henry de Salis *Bradshaw's Canals and Rivers of England and Wales* Blacklock 1904 (David & Charles)
Andrew Shirley *The Published Mezzotints of D Lucas after John Constable R A..*Oxford 1930
Alastair Smart and Attfield Brooks *Constable and his Country* Elak 1976
Keith Turner *Constable Country* The National Trust 2000
Victoria County History Essex:
Volume 2 *Ecclesiastical, Political, Social and Economic* 'Dedham: Queen Elizabeth's Grammar School' 1907 pp. 538-541
Volume 10 *Lexden Hundred* 2002 'Dedham' pp. 154-186 and 'Langham' pp. 242-259
Ambrose J Waller *The Suffolk Stour* Adland 1957
Ian Yearsley *Dedham, Flatford and East Bergholt: A Pictorial History* Phillimore 1996
Dedham Village Photograph Collection Courtesy of Michael and Lucy Archer
Essex Mills Unpublished notes. Courtesy of Duncan Brechels
Simmons Collection and unpublished notes Courtesy of Peter Dolman
Stratford St.Mary Parish Photograph Collection Courtesy of Mary Toone